Crikey I'm...

30

Crikey I'm...™

30

Contributors

Dr David Haslam
Victoria Warner
Eliza Williams

Edited by

Steve Hare

Cover Illustration by

Ian Pollock

PURPLE HOUSE

Published by Purple House Limited 1998
75 Banbury Road
Oxford OX2 6PE

© Purple House Limited 1998

Cover illustration: © Ian Pollock/The Inkshed

Crikey I'm... is a trademark of Purple House
Limited

A catalogue record for this book is available
from the British Library

ISBN 1-84118-012-2

Printed in Great Britain by
Cox and Wyman

Acknowledgements

We are grateful to everyone who helped in the compilation of this book, particularly to the following:

Stephen Franks of Franks and Franks (Design)

Inform Group Worldwide (Reproduction)

Dave Kent of the Kobal Collection

Bodleian Library, Oxford

Central Library, Oxford

British Film Institute

Office of National Statistics

Liz Brown

Mark McClintock

Hannah Wren

Illustrations

Contents

Crikey, I'm 30!

Reaching the round numbers of 10 and 20 posed no threats: you felt each time like you had achieved something. Hitting 30 is somehow altogether different; other people expect some tangible achievement to show for all those years.

If you haven't been there, done that, it's beginning to look like you never will. There are more serious agendas to attend to these days: career, relationships, mortgages – children. Biological clocks have acquired an audible and increasingly insistent tick.

Life, which always seemed to be just for fun, suddenly got serious. And the incessant, supposedly amusing comments of friends and acquaintances reminding you of the fact offers scant reassurance, and does little to dispel the suspicion that you have reached an important milestone.

It's time to give serious reconsideration to your wardrobe, your prospects and your body. Time to make some resolutions, to buy magazines with question marks in the title, to examine yourself with a slightly critical eye.

But it is not the end of life as you know it; rather a new beginning.

It is also not the start of a gradual and inevitable decline into decrepitude and decay that your (younger) friends gleefully describe.

Statistically, if not actually, you are some considerable way short of halfway there. You're at your peak, physically, mentally and emotionally.

This book aims to help you maintain that edge: to welcome the future while celebrating the 30 full years you've already enjoyed.

'You're the one that I want' – Olivia Newton-John and
John Travolta in *Grease*, 1978.

Famous Contemporaries

Cindy Crawford, model, born 20/2/66

Samantha Fox, glamour model and singer, born 15/4/66

Sally Gunnell, athlete, born 29/7/66

Nick Leeson, Barings rogue trader, born 25/2/67

Philip Treacy, fashion designer, born 26/5/67

Paul Gascoigne, footballer, born 27/5/67

Noel Gallagher, musician, born 29/5/67

Pamela Anderson, actor, born 1/7/67

Ulrika Jonsson, television personality, born 16/8/67

Boris Becker, tennis player, born 22/11/67

Patsy Kensit, actor, born 4/3/68

Nasser Hussain, cricketer, born 28/3/68

Kylie Minogue, singer and actor, born 28/5/68

Gillian Anderson, actor, born 9/8/68

Philippa Forrester, television presenter, born 20/9/68

Jason Donovan, entertainer, born 3/6/68

Michael Schumacher, racing driver, born 3/1/69

Karen Brady, managing director of Birmingham City Football Club, born 4/4/69

Mark Ramprakash, cricketer, born 5/9/69

Andi Peters, children television producer and presenter, born 29/7/70

Matt Damon, actor, born 8/10/70

Frankie Dettorri, jockey, born 15/12/70

Gary Barlow, singer, born 20/1/71

Ewan McGregor, actor, born 31/3/71

Winona Ryder, actor, born 29/10/71

Are You a Reincarnation of...?

Yuri Gagarin, cosmonaut, died 27/3/68
Martin Luther King, civil rights activist, died 4/4/68
Robert Kennedy, politician, died 6/6/68
Tony Hancock, comedian, died 24/6/68
Enid Blyton, author, died 28/11/68
John Steinbeck, author, died 20/12/68
John Wyndham, author, died 11/3/69
Judy Garland, singer and actor, died 22/6/69
Brian Jones, musician, died 2/7/69
Otto Dix, artist, died 25/7/69
Ho Chi Minh, North Vietnamese statesman, died 3/9/69
Jack Kerouac, author, died 21/10/69
Bertrand Russell, philosopher, died 2/2/70
Mark Rothko, artist, died 25/2/70
E.M. Forster, author, died 7/6/70
Sir Allen Lane, Penguin publisher, died 7/7/70
Jimi Hendrix, musician, died 18/9/70
Charles de Gaulle, French statesman, died 9/11/70
Gabrielle 'Coco' Chanel, fashion designer, died 10/1/71
Harold Lloyd, comedian and actor, died 8/3/71
Igor Stravinsky, composer, died 6/4/71
Louis Armstrong, musician, died 6/7/71
Nikita Khrushchev, Soviet statesman, died 11/9/71
John Edgar Hoover, US FBI chief, died 2/5/72
C. Day Lewis, poet and novelist, died 22/5/72
Geoffrey Francis Fisher, Archbishop of Canterbury
1945–61, died 14/9/72
Ezra Pound, poet, died 1/11/72
Harry S. Truman, US President 1945–53, died 26/12/72

Children love Cadbury's Milk Chocolate Buttons

Milk Chocolate Buttons are full of nothing but goodness. Just creamy dairy milk in pure Cadbury's chocolate.
No wonder they love them.
It's never too early to start a child on Cadbury's Milk Chocolate Buttons... well, is it?

Cadbury's advertise their chocolate buttons in 1968.

Thirty Somethings

A Look at the World Thirty Years Ago

There's no getting away from it: the late sixties to early seventies, when you were born, was one hell of a time. Your parents, as is *de rigeur*, may well affect no memories at all of the preceding decade and their part in it. Unless, God forbid, they were 'straights'.

From the mid–sixties on, London was the right place at the right time. Young was the only age to be, and art school the only place to study. Britain had it all: fashion, music, beautiful people, even a motor industry. Minis were the only cars to own – Mini Mokes for the most trendy. King's Road and Carnaby Street were not just clichés then. Provincials made pilgrimages to Biba and Habitat.

By the age of 30, you will have spent an average of 1.4 years eating.

Musically, it was never better. Even from the midst of bitter wrangles and the financial farce of their Apple Corps, the Beatles were still producing sublime music, which was rivalled, and occasionally bettered, by the Stones. All but hardcore folkies were now reconciled to an electric Dylan. Then there were the Beach Boys, Van Morrison, The Band,

'For a young man a woman of thirty has irresistible attractions.'
Balzac, *The Woman of Thirty*, 1832

The Doors, The Who, Traffic, The Small Faces, The Kinks, Pink Floyd, Peter Green's Fleetwood Mac, Cream. And the brief meteors of Jimi Hendrix, Janis Joplin, Brian Jones. Such lists go on and on. There were light shows and sitars, never-ending drum solos; it was a time of double albums and gatefold sleeves – necessary, so it was said, for rolling ever-larger joints. If America could boast Woodstock, we had the Isle of Wight, and Reading which, in those days, was still the Jazz & Blues Festival, held at Plumpton.

People sang about 'orange skies, carnivals in cotton candy...'; 'I climbed on the back of a giant albatross...' (this was before *Monty Python*). Everyone talked about 'psychedelic'. Everything was 'cool', unless it was a 'hassle', man. 'What did you do there? I got high!'

On stage, screen and in the street inhibitions were stripped away. With the removal of the Lord Chancellor's powers of stage censorship, shows

30 year-olds watch an average of 21.5 hours of TV per week.

like *Hair* and *Oh Calcutta!* flaunted their newly-won nudity and ephemeral relevance.

There was love and peace. Strange and exotic odours in the air. Clothes of extraordinary hilarity. Rank Afghan coats. Loon pants. Tie-dye and cheesecloth. Your parents went to Stonehenge, read books about ecology, and Mervyn Peake, Tolkien, Hermann

8

Hesse, as well as the minimally titled magazines, *IT* and *Oz*: typography on acid. They bought LPs on the cheap through an ad in *Student* or *Melody Maker* for a tiny company called Virgin.

> 'After 30, a body has a mind of its own.'
>
> Bette Midler

Pirate Radio had been scuppered by the Marine Broadcasting Act of 1967, and the dulcet tones of Tony Blackburn introduced the new establishment and – apart from John Peel, who was cool – straight Radio 1. The Light Programme, Third Programme and Home Service became Radios 2, 3 and 4. Colour televisions began to appear on sale, costing almost exactly the same as they do today.

Meanwhile, in the real world, Vietnam continued as a focus and a unifying force among a disaffected student population, concerned with more than the vagaries of fashion and occasional coastal confrontations between Mods and Rockers. Sordid euphemisms and jargon filled the press briefings of the American military talking coldly about 'VC', 'defoliation' and napalm in an escalating conflict that could never be 'won'. Lieutenant Calley, perpetrator of the Mylai massacre reported, inevitably, that he 'was only following orders'. A grotesque statistic was reported in Congress: that the cost of killing each Vietnamese guerrilla was $400,000.

To every parent with a child over 4*
Lego makes
three Christmas promises

A Lego play will help your child develop his talents. As he plays he learns. Learns about concentration and patience. Learns to use his imagination. Lego play stretches the muscles of a growing mind—makes children brighter.

B Lego will give hours, days, months, years of happy play. (It can build a thousand different toys!) That means fiddledy fingers out of mischief and a blissful hush round the house.

C Lego is one toy that will NOT be broken by Boxing Day. Nor by Boxing Day 1966! Lego bricks are tough, bright and clean and they keep their intriguing power to fit together.

THE BEST SET FOR A CHILD TO START WITH IS PRICED AT 8/-. OTHER SETS RANGE FROM 10/6 TO 105/-. COMPLETE TOWN PLAN SET £7.19.6.

✻ *The upper age limit for Lego! Don's age. A 4 year old makes simple things, an 11 year old builds more complete models. And Lego is for girls, of course, every bit as much as boys.*

Lego advertise for Christmas, 1968.

Smaller conflicts flared up in Nigeria, where Biafran rebels were literally starved into submission. The growing unease between Israel and Arab states which had flared up into the brief 1967 Six-Day War now manifested itself in small acts of terrorism: hijacked aeroplanes, and, in 1972, the attack on Israel's Olympic compound at Munich. In 1971, civil war broke out in Pakistan, over the breakaway state of Bangladesh, which soon involved India in the conflict, and George Harrison in the benefit concert.

> By the age of 30, your heart has beaten an average of 1.1 billion times.

And closer to home, British soldiers, drafted into Ulster in 1969, suffered their first casualty in 1971. The IRA took their campaign to the British mainland, bombing the Post Office Tower. The following year, January's 'Bloody Sunday' saw 13 civil rights marchers shot and killed by British troops. Aldershot was bombed by the IRA the following month, and Prime Minister Edward Heath imposed direct rule on Ulster.

The attitudes of left-wing students to the theory and practice of Communism – nurtured on the exploits of Che Guevara and the Viet Cong – were forced into difficult realignments.

> 'The thirties are a difficult age. Life is finished, living begins.'
>
> A. Bay

Discussion went on into the early hours, in the face of China's Cultural Revolution, the end of the Prague Spring, and Russian tanks rolling through Czechoslovakia, threatening never to stop. Universities sat in. Paris students tore up the cobbles and rioted: 'Street Fighting Man' indeed.

> **By the age of 30, you will have blinked an average of 165 million times.**

Race riots surfaced on a small scale in Notting Hill, and in huge and often fatal conflagrations across the United States. In November 1968 a creepy guy called Richard Nixon replaced Lyndon Johnson in the White House. Martin Luther King and Bobby Kennedy were assassinated the same year. Even Andy Warhol was shot and wounded.

The sixties, hippies, and beautiful people all ended with the bizarre murder of Sharon Tate and her companions by the Charles Manson 'family'. Manson claimed to be acting on instructions interpreted from the lyrics of the Beatles' 'Helter Skelter'. The murder of a fan by a Hell's Angel bouncer at the Stones' Altamont concert was the final straw.

> **30 year-olds spend an average of £2.40 on the National Lottery per week.**

Dr Martens selling their AirWair in 1968.

But there were other distractions. An American took a stroll on the moon in July 1969. In the same year Concorde broke the sound barrier, and the first human egg was fertilised in a test tube.

Following Christiaan Barnard's 1967 pioneering heart transplant, British surgeons the following year transplanted a heart, as well as livers and lungs, though with little initial success.

The first decimal coins appeared, including the ungainly, angular 50 pence pieces replacing the much loved ten-bob note. And people learned to ask for 'four star' instead of 'super' at garages.

In 1968, Rupert Murdoch acquired a controlling interest in *The News of the World* and the following year bought the broadsheet *Sun*, turning it into a tabloid.

In 1970 parliament passed a bill establishing the concept of equal pay for women. The Gay Liberation Front was formed, the Carpenters sang *We've Only Just Begun*, and Sacha Distel sang *Raindrops Keep Falling on My Head*.

> 'At 30 a man should know himself like the palm of his hand, know the exact number of his defects and qualities, know how far he can go, foretell his failures – be what he is. And above all accept these things.'
>
> Albert Camus, *Carnets*, 1942–51

1971 saw Idi Amin take over Uganda. Britain was finally fully decimalised and the first steps taken towards British membership of the Common Market. The Open University was launched on Britain's airwaves. An American company called Intel patented the microprocessor, and the first pocket calculators were introduced. The first IBM personal computer was still ten years away. Princess Anne was voted Sportswoman of the Year, and was spotted in the very latest fashion, hot pants.

At 30, you will have produced an average of 16,000 litres of urine.

In 1972, after his historic visit to China, and the no-less historic visit of his associates to the Watergate complex, Nixon was re-elected in a landslide victory. American troops withdrew gracelessly from Vietnam.

Your parents tuned in to *The Old Grey Whistle Test*, unless they were blacked out during the miners' strike, and maybe even played 'Pong', the first computer game, consisting of two straight lines and a moving dot on a monochrome screen. Wild times and free love were well and truly over.

During an average week, 30 year-olds spend 58 hours asleep; 37 hours on free time; 30 hours in paid work; 21 hours in domestic work; 19 hours in personal care; 3 hours on household maintenance. They have an average of 5 hours' free time on a weekday and 7 hours of free time on a weekend day.

Electronic desk-top personal calculator

How things have changed – calculator technology in 1969.

What Happened When

A Brief Review of the Last Thirty Years

1970

• Strikes by dockers, national newspapers, and local authorities throughout the year in Britain.

• The age of adulthood is reduced in Britain from 21 to 18.

• The Beatles officially split.

• The Gay Liberation Front is formed.

• *The Female Eunuch* by Germaine Greer is published.

1971

• The first British soldier is killed in Ulster since troops entered in 1969.

• Decimal currency is introduced in Britain.

• *Jesus Christ Superstar*, the first musical by Tim Rice and Andrew Lloyd Webber is performed in New York.

• *The Godfather* (directed by Francis Ford Coppola) is released.

1972

• British troops kill 13 in Londonderry's 'Bloody Sunday' after a civil rights march turns into a riot.

• Miner's strikes over pay claims cause blackouts across Britain.

• Nixon aides are arrested for trying to bug the Democrat headquarters in the Watergate complex in the run up to the presidential elections. Nixon denies any responsibility and is re-elected.

• The Race Relations Act comes into force in Britain –

employers can no longer discriminate on the grounds of colour.

• Nike is formed in the US by Phil Knight and Bill Bowerman. They buy the swoosh logo from student Carolyn Davidson for $35.

• 'Pong', the first computer game, is available.

1973

• Britain officially joins the EEC.

• VAT is introduced in Britain.

• The oil states raise the price of oil in the West as a response to US intervention in the Yom Kippur war in the Middle East.

• 'Glam Rock', featuring artists such as Gary Glitter, T-Rex and Elton John, is popular.

1974

• Nixon resigns after admitting to participation in the Watergate scandal. He is the first US President to resign.

• Mohammed Ali beats George Foreman against the odds in Zaire's 'Rumble in the Jungle' to become world heavyweight champion again.

• Lord Lucan disappears after allegedly murdering his nanny and attacking his estranged wife.

• Inflation soars by 20% in Britain.

• IRA bombings of public houses in Guildford (killing 5, injuring 65) and Birmingham (killing 21, injuring 120) cause The Prevention of Terrorism Act to be passed, giving police the right to hold suspects for five days without charge.

1975

• The war in Vietnam is over as Saigon is taken by the North

An early example of the tabloid *Sun* – the format celebrates its thirtieth birthday in 1999.

The book behind the controversial movie – first published in 1971.

Vietnamese and all US troops are withdrawn.

• 'The Guildford Four' and 'The Birmingham Six' are sentenced to life imprisonment.

• Bill Gates, aged 19, and a friend form the Microsoft computer company.

• *Jaws* (directed by Steven Spielberg) is released.

1976

• The first commercial Concorde flights leave from London (for Bahrain) and Paris (for Rio de Janeiro).

• A boiling British summer leads to the instigation of the Droughts Bill to tackle water shortages.

• Fierce race riots take place at the Notting Hill Carnival.

• The Royal National Theatre opens on London's South Bank.

1977

• Elvis Presley dies a suspected drug-related death at his mansion Graceland, in Memphis, US.

• Two homosexual men die and are thought to be the first AIDS (Acquired Immune Deficiency Syndrome) victims in New York, following the diagnosis of the rare cancer Karposi's sarcoma.

• *Star Wars* (directed by George Lucas) is released.

• Punk Music is prominent and projects The Sex Pistols, The Clash, The Jam and Iggy Pop to fame.

1978

• Sid Vicious is charged with murdering his girlfriend Nancy Spungen in New York. He dies of a heroin overdose less than four months later.

1979

• Vietnamese forces seize control of Cambodia, overthrowing the Khmer Rouge. Pol Pot's killing fields are discovered – it is believed that 3–4 million have been murdered or starved to death under his regime.

• Idi Amin flees Uganda following the invasion of the capital, Kampala, by the Tanzanian-backed Uganda Liberation Army. Amin's flight follows years of murder and tyranny.

• Margaret Thatcher becomes the first female British Prime Minister.

• Lord Mountbatten is killed at home in Ireland by an IRA bomb.

1980s

1980

• Drought and war leads to ten million people facing famine in East Africa.

• John Lennon is shot dead outside his apartment building in New York by obsessive fan Mark Chapman.

• 'Who shot JR?' (J. R. Ewing in Dallas) discussions take place across Britain's media: it is revealed in November that Kirsten did it.

• The Olympic Games held in Moscow, USSR are boycotted by 65 countries following the Soviet invasion of Afghanistan.

• The Rubik's Cube becomes a puzzle phenomenon. The object of the game is to create a uniform colour on each side of the cube.

1981

• The 'Yorkshire Ripper', Peter Sutcliffe, is arrested for the murder of 13 women.

• Ten IRA hunger strikers die in the Maze prison, protesting for the right to be segregated from Loyalist supporters in jail.

• Riots and looting break out in Brixton and across the country owing to racial tension, unemployment and poor housing.

• Prince Charles and Lady Diana Spencer marry, watched by 700 million television viewers worldwide.

• *Chariots of Fire* (directed by Hugh Hudson) is released.

1982

• Argentina invade and capture the Falkland Islands but are defeated by the British troops after a two-month war.

• Channel 4 goes on air in Britain. The first programme is the quiz show *Countdown*.

• 20,000 women protest against the planned siting of 96 US Cruise missiles at Greenham Common.

• *Gandhi* (directed by Lord Richard Attenborough) is released.

1983

• Reagan proposes the 'Star Wars' defence system, consisting of a missile shield in space across the US to protect them from Russian attack.

• The pound coin comes into circulation.

• *The Colour Purple* by Alice Walker is published.

1984

• Jayne Torvill and Christopher Dean win an Olympic gold medal for their ice dancing to Ravel's *Bolero*.

• Concern grows over the 'greenhouse effect', where excess carbon dioxide is heating up the earth's atmosphere.

Early days for Paul Weller – The Jam's *In The City*, released in 1977.

- A nationwide miner's strike, led by Arthur Scargill follows low pay increases and the beginning of pit closures.
- Carl Lewis from the USA wins four gold medals in the athletics at the Olympics held in Los Angeles.
- An IRA bomb blasts the Tory conference HQ in Brighton killing four people but narrowly missing Margaret Thatcher.
- A group of international singers form Band Aid and release *Do They Know It's Christmas* to raise money to help the famine victims in Africa. It becomes one of the biggest-selling singles of all time.
- Yuppies, 'Young Upwardly Mobile People', are everywhere.

1985

- Football violence instigated by British fans occurs across Britain and Europe. A fire kills 40 fans in the main stand of Bradford City football ground. Over 40 Britons and Italians are killed when a safety wall collapses in Brussels' Heysel Stadium.
- Boris Becker beats Kevin Curren 6:3 6:7 7:6 6:4 in the men's singles at Wimbledon to become the first German and first unseeded player to win.
- Bob Geldof organises the 'Live Aid' concert in aid of Africa at Wembley Stadium and raises £50 million.
- The World Health Organisation announces that AIDS has reached epidemic proportions.

1986

- The American space shuttle *Challenger* explodes seconds after take-off killing all aboard, including school teacher volunteer Christa McAuliffe.
- Riots take place between black youths and police in black

townships in South Africa. All reporters and television crews are kept out.

• Argentina beat Belguim 3–2 in the World Cup. They knock England out in the quarter-finals with help from Maradona's 'hand of God'.

• Radiation is released during a fire at Chernobyl nuclear reactor in Russia.

1987

• 187 die as *The Herald of Free Enterprise* ferry sinks leaving Zeebrugge when the bow doors are not shut properly.

• Michael Ryan shoots 16 dead including his mother, in Hungerford, and then shoots himself.

• The stock market falls by 10 per cent on 'Black Monday' causing the worst crash this century.

• 6,000 emergency calls are made to the Fire Brigade in 24 hours during and after the worst storm this century in England, which causes between £100 million and £600 million worth of damage and kills 18 people.

• 30 die in a fire at King's Cross tube station.

• Reagan and Gorbachev sign a mutual agreement to cut the size of their nuclear weapons.

1988

• Soviet Perestroika goes into effect, transferring a large portion of economic responsibility from the government to individual enterprises.

• Pan Am flight 103 from London to New York crashes in Lockerbie, Scotland, killing all aboard in suspected terrorist-bombing.

• *A Brief History of Time* by Stephen Hawking is published.

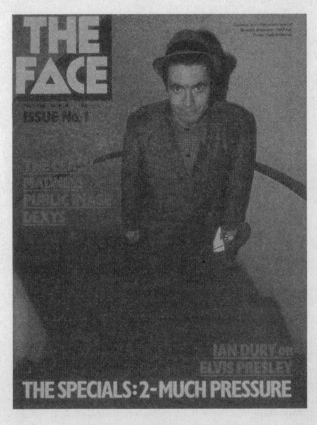

The first issue of *The Face*, 1980.

1989

• Salman Rushdie is condemned to death for blasphemy by Iran's Ayatollah Ruhollah Khomeini following publication of *The Satanic Verses*.

• 94 fans die in the Hillsborough stadium disaster in Sheffield after fans are crushed when too many are let in.

• Tanks roll into Tiananmen Square in China and crush democracy attempts, killing more than 2,000 people.

• 'The Guildford Four' are released from jail after serving 14 years for wrongful convictions of IRA bombing attacks on pubs in Guildford in 1974.

• The Berlin Wall is pulled down, symbolising the end of Soviet international communism.

• Ceausescu, the Romanian dictator, and his wife are executed after being found guilty by a people's court of attempting to crush demonstrations against the communist government.

• Acid House rave parties in the open air attract thousands of young people, despite clampdowns by police.

1990s

1990

• The government gives £2.2 million for research into BSE, known as 'mad cow disease'. The Commons Agriculture Committee says there is no evidence to suggest a threat to human health.

• Authorities in South Africa lift the 30-year ban on the ANC (African National Congress) and Nelson Mandela is released from jail.

• East and West Germany are reunified.

- Thatcher resigns as British PM to be replaced by John Major.

1991

- The Gulf War begins after Iraqi troops refuse to withdraw from Kuwait by the deadline given by the UN.
- The 'Birmingham Six' are released from jail after serving 16 years for IRA bombing of pubs in Birmingham in 1974 that they did not commit.
- A videotape reveals four Los Angeles police officers beating black motorist Rodney King and causes outcry in the US.
- Apartheid collapses in South Africa after the repeal of Land Acts, Group Areas Act and Population Registration Act.
- Civil war breaks out in Yugoslavia between Serbs, Croats and Muslims.

1992

- Rioting and looting take place across Los Angeles following the acquittal of the policemen involved in the Rodney King case.
- Windsor Castle is badly damaged by fire, rounding off the Queen's *annus horribilis*.

1993

- Two ten year-old boys are arrested and found guilty of the murder of toddler James Bulger.
- The European Union is formed with the implementation of the Maastricht treaty.
- Rachel Whiteread receives the Turner Prize for *House*, a concrete cast of the inside of a house. She also receives an award for 'Worst Artist of the Year' from the K Foundation.

1994

• The Church of England decides to ordain seven women priests.

• Frederick and Rosemary West are charged with the murder of eight women whose bodies are found in the garden of their house.

• Following the sudden death of John Smith, Tony Blair becomes the leader of the Labour opposition party.

• The Channel Tunnel opens between Britain and France.

• Nelson Mandela is inaugurated as South Africa's first black President.

• O. J. Simpson leads police cars and TV reporters on a car chase across Los Angeles after failing to appear for an arraignment on charges of murdering his former wife Nicole and her friend Ronald Goldman.

• £7 million is spent on the first day of UK Lottery sales.

1995

• Nick Leeson, 28, is arrested in Germany for causing the collapse of Barings Bank by gambling on high risk derivatives on the Singapore market.

• O. J. Simpson is found not guilty of murder.

• Princess Diana gives a television interview on *Panorama* revealing her affair with James Hewitt and her feelings about her marriage. The Queen consequently urges Charles and Diana to divorce.

• The rise of 'Brit Pop' with chart wars between Blur, Oasis, Pulp, Supergrass...

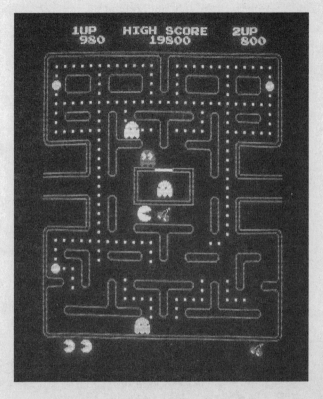

Pac-Man gobbled his way to fame in 1982.

Thirty One Hit Wonders

1960	Ricky Valance: *Tell Laura I Love Her*
1962	B. Bumble and the Stingers: *Nut Rocker*
1966	Overlanders: *Michelle*
1968	Crazy World of Arthur Brown: *Fire*
1969	Zagar and Evans: *In The Year 2525*
1969	Jane Birkin and Serge Gainsbourg: *Je t'aime.../Moi Non Plus*
1969	Archies: *Sugar Sugar*
1970	Lee Marvin: *Wand'rin' Star*
1970	Norman Greenbaum: *Spirit in the Sky*
1970	Matthews' Southern Comfort: *Woodstock*
1971	Clive Dunn: *Grandad*
1973	Simon Park Orchestra: *Eye Level*
1975	Typically Tropical: *Barbados*
1976	J. J. Barrie: *No Charge*
1977	Floaters: *Float On*
1978	Althia and Donna: *Up Town Top Ranking*
1978	Brian and Michael: *Matchstalk Men and Matchstalk Cats and Dogs*
1979	Anita Ward: *Ring My Bell*
1979	Lena Martell: *One Day At A Time*
1980	Fern Kinney: *Together We Are Beautiful*
1980	MASH: *Theme From M*A*S*H*
1980	St Winifred's School Choir: *There's No One Quite Like Grandma*
1981	Joe Dolce Music Theatre: *Shaddap You Face*
1982	Charlene: *I've Never Been To Me*
1985	Phyllis Nelson: *Move Closer*
1987	M/A/R/R/S: *Pump Up The Volume*
1988	Robin Beck: *First Time*
1990	Partners In Kryme: *Turtle Power*
1991	Hale & Pace and the Stonkers: *The Stonk*
1994	Doop: *Doop*

Information from *Guinness British Hit Singles* 11th edition
© 1995 Guinness Publishing Ltd.

Mel Gibson stars in the futuristic *Mad Max*, 1979.

Old At Thirty

Thirty Then and Now

As a new 30 year-old, your peak of physical fitness lies ahead. Career-wise as well, the path is still uphill; you may only have been out of higher education for a short time, and you still have some way to go yet before you fulfil all your ambitions. If you have children, they are likely to be quite small: certainly you wouldn't class yourself as old – all the time in the world remains in store, because you have, on average, another 40 years of life left.

Pity, then, your average 30 year-old 250 years ago. Living in a town, as an affluent individual, you'd have just 13 years left (the average lifespan being 43). As a tradesman, you'd be expected to pop your clogs any day now (the average lifespan being 30); and as a labourer, you'd probably have shuffled off this mortal coil some eight years ago. If you think that's bad, consider the situation in the seventeenth century: as a poor person, you lived for just 18 years on average; even if you were rich, you probably only made it to

Thirty: Unlucky for Some...

Some people regard 30 as an unlucky number: Judas was given 30 pieces of silver as a fee for betraying Jesus to the Romans. Judas never actually used the money, however; instead he flung it at the feet of the priests, before hanging himself. The holy men used it to buy a field, which would serve as a graveyard for foreigners.

the age of 22.

Forget worrying about work, the mortgage, the kids or your social life; back in the seven-

At the age of 30, you will have grown an average of 11 metres of finger nails.

teenth century, one of the biggest problems facing a 30 year-old was disease. Scrofula was particularly virulent in those days: it was a kind of tuberculosis of the lymph glands. A sure sign that you had it was when the glands on your neck swelled to twice the normal size and started oozing. Not to worry, though – many people firmly believed that scrofula could be completely cured if the monarch laid his/her hands on you. In Norfolk, some people still believed in the healing powers of the sovereign until the middle of this century.

If the scrofula didn't get you, however, pulmonary tuberculosis almost certainly would – rates of infection in towns during the seventeenth century were very high. In 1685, according to one writer at the time, up to a fifth of all deaths in London were due to tuberculosis.

Anyway, imagine you've somehow managed to defy the odds, and have reached your thirtieth birthday in the seventeenth or eighteenth century. Would you be married with dozens of children? Not necessarily. Many men of the working classes – or the younger sons of the richer classes, who didn't inherit – had to wait until they were financially secure before they could marry, which could be as late as 30. Naturally, some people married earlier, otherwise – given the low life expectancy – the population would have been in a pretty dire state; but generally speaking, the longer you could wait the better.

As a woman, chances are you would be married, although women didn't generally get married until their early or mid twenties – not quite as early as you would expect. As for children, a lack of contraceptive methods meant that by the age of 30 you would almost certainly have several. Because of high infant mortality, you could have given birth to as many as seven or eight children, but only three or four would be likely to survive. Don't worry, though – at the age of about 40 (ten or so years earlier than now), you'd be entering the menopause. Providing, again, that you made it that far.

Suddenly, the twentieth century seems like a much nicer place in which to turn 30!

The stables of King Augias had not been cleaned for 30 years and contained 3000 oxen when Hercules was asked to clean them. He agreed to do it, on the condition that he was given one-tenth of the oxen. Stomach churning, Hercules diverted the rivers Alpheus and Peneius to make them run through the stables and wash them out; although the King never did give him the promised oxen.

Bagpuss – 'When Bagpuss goes to sleep, all the animals go to sleep'.

Do You Remember...?

Blasts from the Past

Record Breakers – hosted by Roy Castle and Norris McWhirter. Roy Castle broke the tap-dancing and parascending records during the show.

Think of a Number

John Craven's Newsround

We Are The Champions

Grange Hill

Rentaghost – the Meaker family, Timothy Claypole, Nadia Popov and the Pantomime Horse amongst others.

Worzel Gummidge

Paddington

Mr Ben

Take Hart – featuring Morph and Mr Bennett.

Blue Peter – writers of outstanding letters and competition winners would receive a Blue Peter badge; writers of exceptional environmental letters would receive a green Blue Peter badge. Gold badges would be given for outstanding achievement.

Rainbow – with singers Rod, Jane and Freddie along with Zippy, George and Bungle.

Tiswas – hosted by Chris Tarrant, Sally James and Lenny Henry. Featured the Phantom Flan Flinger and lots of gunge. It was first billed in the *TV Times* as: 'If you want culture, education, serious discussion and politics you won't find it here. But if you want slapstick, cartoons, animals, pop stars and hundreds nay millions of – well two or three anyway – hysterically funny jokes then this is the space to watch.'

Multi-Coloured Swap Shop – hosted by Noel Edmonds with Keith Chegwin doing the outside broadcasts. Also featured were Posh Paws the purple dinosaur and the invisible Eric who lowered the bundles of competition entries.

Animal Magic

Cheggers Plays Pop

'Boom! Boom!' – Basil Brush, in his prime.

The Police – *Message in a Bottle* and *Walking on the Moon* reached No. 1 in 1979; *Don't Stand So Close To Me* reached No. 1 in 1980.

Blondie – *The Tide is High*, *Atomic* and *Call Me* reached No. 1 in 1980.

Adam Ant – *Stand and Deliver* and *Prince Charming* reached No. 1 in 1980, *Goody Two Shoes* reached No. 1 in 1982.

Madness – *My Girl* reached No. 3 in 1980, *House of Fun* reached No. 1 in 1982.

Abba – *The Winner Takes it All* and *Super Trouper* reached No. 1 in 1980.

The Specials – *The Special AKA Live!* reached No. 1 in 1980, *Ghost Town* reached No. 1 in 1981.

The Jam – *Going Underground* and *Start* reached No. 1 in 1980, *A Town Called Malice* and *Beat Surrender* reached No. 1 in 1982.

Bucks Fizz – *Making Your Mind Up* reached No. 1 in 1981, *Land Of Make Believe* and *My Camera Never Lies* reached No. 1 in 1982.

Human League – *Don't You Want Me* reached No. 1 in 1981.

Soft Cell – *Tainted Love* reached No. 1 in 1981.

David Essex – *A Winter's Tale* reached No. 2 in 1982.

Culture Club – *Do You Really Want To Hurt Me?* reached No. 1 in 1982, *Karma Chameleon* reached No. 1 in 1983.

Tight Fit – *The Lion Sleeps Tonight* reached No. 1 in 1982.

Captain Sensible – *Happy Talk* reached No. 1 in 1982.

Wham! – *Young Guns (Go For It)* reached No. 3 in 1982, *Wake Me Up Before You Go Go* and *Freedom* reached No. 1 in 1984.

Irene Cara – *Fame* reached No. 1 in 1982.

Musical Youth – *Pass the Dutchie* reached No. 1 in 1982.

Michael Jackson – *Billie Jean* reached No. 1, *Beat It* reached No. 3 and *Thriller* reached No. 10 in 1983.

Duran Duran – *Is There Something I Should Know?* reached No. 1 in 1983, *The Reflex* reached No. 1 in 1984.

Spandau Ballet – *True* reached No. 1 in 1983.

Paul Young – *Wherever I Lay My Hat (That's My Home)* reached No. 1 in 1983.

Men At Work – *Down Under* reached No. 1 in 1983.

Flying Pickets – *Only You* reached No. 1 in 1983.

Dexy's Midnight Runners – *Geno* reached No. 1 in 1980, *Come On Eileen* reached No. 1 in 1982.

Can You Imagine Life Without...?

Popular Inventions In Your Lifetime

Trivial Pursuit – First exhibited at the International Toy Show in New York in 1982, but was initially unsuccessful. After backing from major distributors Selchow and Righter (their previous successes were Scrabble and Jeopardy), the game became a massive worldwide success in 1984, with little advertising or promotion.

Post-it Notes – Went on sale in the US in 1980 and in Europe in 1981. In 1983, sales totalled $45 million, and for a number of years increased at a reputed growth rate of 85 per cent.

Jacuzzi – Prototype bath first made by Roy Jacuzzi in 1968 as a response to America's health and fitness craze. The two-person tub was first introduced in 1970. It became a trend to go nude bathing in a hot tub in the 1970s and the pastime was frequently shown on TV and in movies.

Filofax – The trademark was first registered in 1930, but it was only internationally marketed in 1972, and by 1980 was hugely successful and something of a trademark for the 1980s.

Video Recorder – Sony introduced the Betamax video player in 1975, while JVC launched their VHS cassette recorder in September 1976. JVC got other Japanese companies to join them, producing only

VHS compatible video recorders, which thus became the standard. Also, JVC were first to introduce the video camera as an accompaniment to the recorder, increasing the appeal by making it interactive. RCA in America also backed VHS over Betamax, thus vastly increasing the success of the product in the US. It was the American market that eventually caused VHS's overwhelming success; by 1985, VHS accounted for more than 80 per cent of the VCR sales in the world and it was becoming difficult for Betamax owners to find tapes, blank or pre-recorded in their format.

Walkman – Launched in the summer of 1979 by Sony. It was originally seen as a failure, as the idea was developed initially as a 'Pressman', a small stereo recording device for journalists. It was too small for a recording mechanism, however, and could only play back tapes. But by 1980, after the vital addition of the headphones, the 'Walkman' was the most popular tape machine ever.

Microwave Oven – First designed by US company Raytheon in 1946, but only became available on the market in 1953 and was almost as large and heavy as a refrigerator. It was redesigned by the Japanese who made it smaller and cheaper, and was marketed by Sharp in 1966/7. In 1968, 30,000 were sold internationally; but by 1985, 15 million had been sold. The slow build up of the microwave's popularity may have been due initially to poor marketing, but also to suspicion and set ways of cooking.

Compact Discs – In 1982, the first CDs and players were launched by Philips. Initially only 150 music titles were made, most of them classical. However, due to popular demand from both buyers and artists, it is now the most common form of music media.

Food Processor – Designed by Frenchman Pierre Vendon in 1971 with a high-speed chopping blade, and electronic speed control.

Fax Machines – Based on an idea patented by Scotsman Alexander Bain in 1843. Huge versions were used by newspapers to send pictures around the world, until one small enough for office use became available in the 1980s.

The Rubik's Cube – Invented by Erno Rubik in 1980; the object of the cubed puzzle being to arrange all the faces with a uniform colour.

Gossard Wonderbra – Gossard have been dealing in corsets and underwear since 1901, but in 1968 they advertised their new girdle with the model wearing a low-cut bra for decency. Contary to their expectations, the girdle was shoved aside in favour of the bra, and the popularity of the wonderbra was born!

Electric Kettle – In 1975, Swan introduced the Swan Automatic, the first fully automatic kettle that switched itself off when the water had boiled, and had a reset button to bring it back to the boil.

A Fit Thirty

Dr David Haslam

This can be a wonderful age. You may well be at the peak of your physical condition, and feeling psychologically more together than at any previous age. Or it can be a time for panic, when you suddenly realise that many of those childhood dreams are drifting out of reach. How many men in their thirties have felt intense relief to find that someone in the national team of their chosen sport is older than they are?

Even though you know you are 30, deep down you still feel exactly the same as when you were 20. It's only when you see a group of genuine 20 year-olds that you realise you've been there, done that, and benefited from the experience.

Your Changing Body
The changes from the twenties to the thirties are subtle, but important.

- At 20 you can abuse your body and seem to get away with it. At 30 you will almost certainly know the next day.

- Your body weight will increase if you don't keep up your activity levels. There is no such thing as middle-age spread, and this isn't the beginning of it. Weight goes on when you take in too much food and drink, and don't do enough exercise to compensate. That's all.

- Your sex drive could be at its height – given the right

Jane Fonda's 1982 book was the exercise bible for a generation.

opportunities. Unfortunately, if you have small children, you will know that they have an amazing sense of timing, and can be a great natural contraceptive if they call out or cry as you are making love. And sex can become boring if you let it. So don't allow it to drift into a habit, about as exciting as doing the ironing. Imagination, time, sensitivity, and love are all it takes.

- For men who are going to lose their hair, the first signs may appear in the thirties, or even earlier. Don't think of it as a receding hairline, more as a prominent forehead. And don't waste your money on potions and lotions.

- Exercise is vital. Keeping fit doesn't entail immediately joining a gym, but if possible, do try to get three sessions a week of real exercise that you enjoy.

- Prevention is always better than cure. Because of contraception or child care, women tend to see doctors fairly frequently and have regular preventative checks. Men tend to wait till they are ill. Do get your blood pressure checked at least every couple of years.

- The most important thing you can do for your health is not smoking. Talk to your doctor if you need help giving up.

- A small amount of alcohol is probably good for the heart, but the absolute weekly maximum should be 28 units for men, and 21 for women – ideally less.

The bike to own in the seventies and early eighties: a
Raleigh Chopper.

Your Changing Emotions

If you are in a career, your thirties may be a time when you feel you must work flat out to reach the top. If you also have young children, however, this is a particularly special period in their lives. For many parents, getting the right balance between work and home is extremely difficult. But don't kid yourself that you can have short spells of 'quality' time. Children need long spells of 'not doing anything very much with their parents' to develop emotionally. And you need it, too.

The average age of a woman giving birth in the UK is now 28 and rising, so increasingly it is couples in their thirties and forties who have young children. However, if you haven't yet had children, your thirties is crunch time for making that decision. Remember that the older you are when you first attempt a pregnancy, the longer it may take to conceive; and the less time there will be for investigations and treatment, if nature doesn't take its course. Alternatively, you may feel deeply relieved that you never had children, even if you are under intolerable family pressure to conform to their expectations. Remember, it's your life, and it's not a rehearsal.

Many people in their thirties suffer from stress-related problems – whether triggered by work, home, or relationships. Make sure you take time out to relax, by yourself, or with a partner; do things you enjoy; buy a relaxation tape; or invest in some aromatherapy oils. Symptoms of severe stress can often be helped with counselling, but if you feel constantly unhappy, with disturbed sleep, poor appetite, loss of interest and enthusiasm, and a reduced sex drive, then you could well be clinically depressed. This is very common, and very treatable. Talk to your doctor now.

For many people, turning 30 makes them feel suddenly very old. They look at our increasingly youth-dominated culture, and feel that they are past it. But the simple fact is that, at 30, chances are you still haven't reached the middle of your life. The average midpoint of life is now 36 years for men, and 39 for women: so you certainly don't need to feel, or act, middle-aged. There's a lot of time left, and a lot for you still to do.

Being 30 does have advantages. At 30 you know many of the things that you wished you'd known when you were younger. You are young enough to have dreams, and should be energetic enough to go for them. If you keep yourself fit, you can be every bit as active as you were in your twenties. If you want being 30 to be an excuse for slowing down or giving up, then it's your decision. But it would be a dreadful waste. Have fun!

David Haslam is married with two children and has been a GP for 22 years. He is a Fellow of the Royal College of General Practitioners, and has written numerous books – the most recent being Stress Free Parenting. *He also writes a column for* Practical Parenting *magazine, and frequently broadcasts on health topics.*

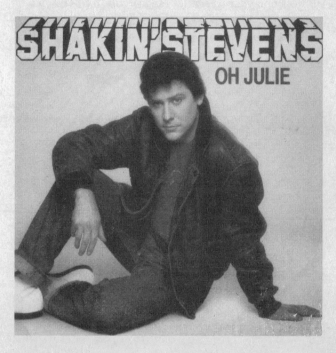

Shakin' Stevens' single *Oh Julie* reached Number One in the charts in 1982 – he went on to enjoy many more chart hits throughout the eighties and into the nineties.

Thirty Wimbledon Winners

Male Winners

1998	Pete Sampras beat Goran Ivanisevic 6:7 7:6 6:4 3:6 6:2
1997	Pete Sampras beat Cedric Pioline 6:4 6:2 6:4
1996	Richard Krajicek beat MaliVai Washington 6:3 6:4 6:3
1995	Pete Sampras beat Boris Becker 6:7 6:2 6:4 6:2
1994	Pete Sampras beat Goran Ivanisevic 7:6 7:6 6:0
1993	Pete Sampras beat Jim Courier 7:6 7:6 3:6 6:3
1992	Andre Agassi beat Goran Ivansevic 6:7 6:4 6:4 1:6 6:4
1991	Micheal Stich beat Boris Becker 6:4 7:6 6:4
1990	Stefan Edberg beat Boris Becker 6:2 6:2 3:6 3:6 6:4
1989	Boris Becker beat Stefan Edberg 6:0 7:6 6:4
1988	Stefan Edberg beat Boris Becker 4:6 7:6 6:4 6:2
1987	Pat Cash beat Ivan Lendl 7:6 6:2 7:5
1986	Boris Becker beat Ivan Lendl 6:4 6:3 7:5
1985	Boris Becker beat Kevin Curren 6:3 6:7 7:6 6:4
1984	John McEnroe beat Jimmy Connors 6:1 6:1 6:2
1983	John McEnroe beat Chris Lewis 6:2 6:2 6:2
1982	Jimmy Connors beat John McEnroe 3:6 6:3 6:7 7:6 6:4
1981	John McEnroe beat Björn Borg 4:6 7:6 7:6 6:4
1980	Björn Borg beat John McEnroe 1:6 7:5 6:3 6:7 8:6
1979	Björn Borg beat Roscoe Tanner 6:7 6:1 3:6 6:3 6:4
1978	Björn Borg beat Jimmy Connors 6:2 6:2 6:3
1977	Björn Borg beat Jimmy Connors 3:6 6:2 6:1 5:7 6:4
1976	Björn Borg beat Ilie Nastase 6:4 6:2 9:7
1975	Arthur Ashe beat Jimmy Connors 6:1 6:1 5:7 6:4
1974	Jimmy Connors beat Ken Rosewall 6:1 6:1 6:4
1973	Jan Kodes beat Alex Metreveli 6:1 9:8 6:3
1972	Stan Smith beat Ilie Nastase 4:6 6:3 6:3 4:6 7:5
1971	John Newcombe beat Stan Smith 6:3 5:7 2:6 6:4 6:4
1970	John Newcombe beat Ken Rosewall 5:7 6:3 6:3 3:6 6:1
1969	Rod Laver beat John Newcombe 6:4 5:7 6:4 6:4

Female Winners

1998	Jana Novotna beat Nathalie Tauziat 6:4 7:6
1997	Martina Hingis beat Jana Novotna 2:6 6:3 6:3
1996	Steffi Graf beat Arantxa Sanchez Vicario 6:3 7:5
1995	Steffi Graf beat Arantxa Sanchez Vicario 4:6 6:1 7:5
1994	Conchita Martinez beat Martina Navratilova 6:4 3:6 6:3
1993	Steffi Graf beat Jana Novotna 7:6 1:6 6:4
1992	Steffi Graf beat Monica Seles 6:2 6:1
1991	Steffi Graf beat Gabriella Sabatini 6:4 3:6 8:6
1990	Martina Navratilova beat Zena Garrison 6:4 6:1
1989	Steffi Graf beat Martina Navratilova 6:2 6:7 6:1
1988	Steffi Graf beat Martina Navratilova 5:7 6:2 6:1
1987	Martina Navratilova beat Steffi Graf 7:5 6:3
1986	Martina Navratilova beat Hana Mandlikova 7:6 6:3
1985	Martina Navratilova beat Chris Evert 4:6 6:3 6:2
1984	Martina Navratilova beat Chris Evert 7:6 6:2
1983	Martina Navratilova beat Andrea Jaeger 6:0 6:3
1982	Martina Navratilova beat Chris Evert 6:1 3:6 6:2
1981	Chris Evert beat Hana Mandlikova 6:2 6:2
1980	Evonne Cawley beat Chris Evert 6:1 7:6
1979	Martina Navratilova beat Chris Evert 6:4 6:4
1978	Martina Navratilova beat Chris Evert 2:6 6:4 7:5
1977	Virginia Wade beat Betty Stove 4:6 6:3 6:1
1976	Chris Evert beat Evonne Cawley 6:3 4:6 8:6
1975	Billie-Jean King beat Evonne Cawley 6:0 6:1
1974	Chris Evert beat Olga Morozova 6:0 6:4
1973	Billie-Jean King beat Chris Evert 6:0 7:5
1972	Billie-Jean King beat Evonne Goolagong 6:3 6:3
1971	Evonne Goolagong beat Margaret Court 6:4 6:1
1970	Margaret Court beat Billie-Jean King 14:12 11:9
1969	Ann Jones beat Billie-Jean King 3:6 6:3 6:2

Top Thirty

Fame Comes To Those Who Wait

Scott of the Antarctic embarked on his voyage to the
Antarctic at the age of 33

•

Amelia Earhart became the first woman to make a trans-
atlantic solo flight at the age of 34

•

James Cagney made his film debut aged 31 in
The Sinner's Holiday

•

Sir Edmund Hillary was 34 when he became the first moun-
taineer to reach the summit of Everest in 1953

•

Dustin Hoffman was 30 when he starred in *The Graduate*

•

Jack Nicholson made *Easy Rider* aged 32

•

Francis Ford Coppola directed *The Godfathe*r aged 33

•

Fred Astaire began his film career aged 34 after retiring
from dancing in music halls

•

Michelangelo Antonioni began making films at the age of
30 after working in a bank

•

Martin Scorsese made his first major film, *Boxcar Bertha*,
aged 30

•

Woody Allen made his first film, *What's New Pussycat?* at
the age of 30

Thomas Hardy wrote his first successful novel *Far From The Madding Crowd* aged 34

•

Beatrix Potter wrote her first children's book *Peter Rabbit* aged 34

•

Jean-Paul Sartre wrote his first novel, *Nausea*, aged 33

•

Vincent Van Gogh began painting in his early 30s

•

Harrison Ford had his first leading role in *Star Wars* at the age of 35

•

Wilbur Wright and **Orville Wright** made their first powered aeroplane flights aged 36 and 33 respectively

•

Sebastian Coe was elected as a Conservative MP aged 32, after his retirement from sport two years previously, following an eight year career as an athlete

•

Carrie Fisher published her first book, *Postcards from the Edge*, aged 31

•

Jarvis Cocker was 31 when his band Pulp finally hit the big time with *His 'n' Hers* in 1994, even though their first album was released in 1983

•

Anita Roddick founded the Body Shop at the age of 34

Copyright Notices